Wild Man of the Mountain

WILD MAN
OF THE
MOUNTAIN

A drama in verse by

TONY HOWARTH

Broadstone

ISBN 978-1-937968-94-6

Text Design by Larry W. Moore
Cover by Stephanie Potter

Broadstone Books
An Imprint of
Broadstone Media LLC
418 Ann Street
Frankfort, KY 40601-1929
BroadstoneBooks.com

At Walden Pond —
as the sun arose, I saw it throwing off its nightly
clothing of mist, and here and there, by degrees, its
soft ripples or its smooth reflecting surface was
revealed, while the mists, like ghosts, were stealthily
withdrawing in every direction, into the woods

—Henry David Thoreau

MOLLY: (*her coffee shop*)

the day he walked in
I wanted to throw him out
torn and scruffy
face and hands
smothered with smudge
looking for a handout
you here for breakfast?

DAG:

oh ya, you bet, an apple
an apple turnover
and, and a coffee
milk, three sugars

MOLLY:

gonna cost you two dollars

DAG:

that's good
I got two dollars
I do I got two dollars
see

MOLLY:

and he put them on the table

~

MOLLY: (*don't call it junk*)

     when I brought the turnover
     he wolfed it
     like somebody might try'n
     snatch it away
     so tell me things
     I seen you
     wandering round town

DAG:

     ya, I do, I wander
     round town
     and all over everywhere else
     looking for stuff
     like this
     ashtray, see how it's cracked
     all around the edge
     somebody threw it away
     but it's still got some
     got some joyful life in it
     like this newspaper
     oh, oh, oh, tear this picture
     out of this newspaper
     and I put it
     put it in the ashtray
     see how the ashtray
     now it's a frame
     a picture frame
     that's what I do
     I turn ashtrays
     into picture frames

MOLLY:

>   you the one
>   caught up in a lawsuit
>   with Ernie Brown?
>   all the junk
>   spilling across his property?

DAG:

>   not *junk*
>   don't call it *junk*
>   don't never call it *junk*

MOLLY:

>   okay, sorry

DAG:

>   creepy shitface
>   he started it
>   calling it *junk*

MOLLY:

>   cool down

DAG:

>   and the judge
>   he called it *junk* too
>   what happen to reverence?
>   what happen to justice?

MOLLY:

> how many times I got to say it
> I'm sorry

DAG:

> I take the stuff I find
> in this fucked-up world
> I make it whole again
> make it belong somewhere

MOLLY:

> and that's anything but junk

DAG:

> ya, but that judge
> nobody ever lets me be
> who I want to be
> see I hated school
> so they give me a test
> what d'you see in the picture
> I say milk
> and they go bananas, no milk
> yes milk cos you got a cow
> look at those horns
> with a cow you get milk
> they flunk me
> so I quit school
> and my father ever after
> calls me birdbrain
> calls me Dag
> all of them call me Dag
> got so I can't remember my baptize name

but so
s'all over now
cos I tumble my treasures
other end of the pond
no flat space any more
but on the edge of a cliff
I keep my dreamland
except that judge
what he said
lamentable
you think that too, don't you
lamentable

MOLLY:

no

DAG:

no?

MOLLY:

don't call it junk
never call it junk
and we laughed

DAG:

look
another two dollars
you got another turnover?

MOLLY:

milk, three sugars?

DAG:

> ya, and thank you
> nice here
> let me sit here
> listening to my side of the story
> people don't do that
> listen
> to my side of the story

~

DAG: (*Dreamland Garden*)

scrounge all over
clawfoot bathtub
next to the banged-up fender
of an old Model T
scar-face angel
always room for an angel
with the frusbee I found
for a halo
un-inter-ruffled bliss
everything here
got a story
this rusty old bedstead
look at its paint
all curling and chunky
maybe a lady
gray hair and sick
wanted precious peace
while she was dying
or an old man alone
got a dog
who crept every night
under the blanket

~

DAG: (*alone but not alone*)

caaaah

well hello, mister crow
or are you momma crow?
hard to tell with a crow
that your favorite spruce tree?
you're not gonna answer?
too busy got a question of your own?
like why is somebody like me
hanging out
under your favorite tree?
twizzle your wings, hop along the branch
what, you want me to talk louder?

caaaah

so, louder — oh, look at that
leaping and darting
wish I could be up there with you
looking down away from what
all the wicked shambles people do
and oh my, look at that
swoop in close
aren't you glad
I put that bedstead?
don't wobble though, do it
like your sprucetree branch

caaaah

I don't speak crow
but thank you
you did just tell me, din't you
what I think you told me?
welcome to Dreamland Garden?

~

MOLLY: (*more gossip*)

    apple turnover
    coffee, three sugars

DAG:

    ya, thanks
    like the sign says
    Molly's Coffeeshop
    are you the Molly?

MOLLY:

    that's me

DAG:

    I got to tell you, Molly
    gonna build a tower
    six stories high
    on top of the cliff
    so I can see over the treetops
    I want to every day wake up
    like how I did today
    good morning doves all around
    cooing to one another
    in the rising sunny shine
    a woodpecker joins in
    tat–tatta-tat, tat–tatta-tat
    a woodchuck plays with her chuckles

MOLLY:

    so I hear you been
    talking to the bank

DAG:

how you know that?
you been spying?

MOLLY:

hey, look around
Molly's Gossipshop

DAG:

ha, thats funny
Molly's Gossipshop

MOLLY:

they tell me they're renovating
I mention it because
they got this giant stain glass window

DAG:

and, and, they ask do I want it
oh, they gonna put it on a truck
bring it all the way up my dirt road
bring it into my dreamland

MOLLY:

nice

DAG:

ya

~

DAG: (*the dream*)

first my tower got to have a foundation
put the stain glass on top of it
a place behind for my hideaway
maybe get lectric lights
power line all along the road
maybe a mattress so I can sleep
wake up with the morning light
wrapping me in red and yellow
a tower so I can watch the eagles
geese when they migrate
gonna watch the sunsets
lightning and trees shake in a storm
inside listen to raindrops
ping-pong on the window glass
the whole world
dancing for me like it never has before
ohhhh

DAG: (*as the tower takes shape*)

thunder

                          rain

    leaks through the roof

                      pummels the window

        sit here   my back   to the glass

    drenched

                          alone

                              listen to trees
                      splinter

    black dark

                  where do birds hide
                      storms like this

    listen to the tower

                          creak

                                      shiver
                  what if it all caves in

        awake

            all night long

    daylight
                      silence

outside

        shattered branches

   broken glass

     Angel

        flat on the ground

~

DAG: (*with Angel*)

all right, my friend
let's get you back the way you were
face stuck in the mud
oh boy, no more nose
scraped flat
got your eye chipped a bit too
kind of wrinkled
gonna make you smile
even when you don't want to
gonna make you smile
oh no, the wing
broke off
oh man
well
tell you what
I got this construction glue
gonna patch up the roof with it
take some of it all sticky
a little dab
on the back of your wing
put you back together
see I know what you been through
Dad bought this land
so he could build a summer cottage
a country getaway next to the pond
cleared the land but never built it
when he died the whole family
wanted nothing to do with it
too rough and treesy
so ha ha dump it on birdbrain
but lookit me laughing back at them

and you laughing with me
this gonna be the jewel
of all these mountains
hold still now
while I stand you up
ya, way to go, brother
good as new
it's happy time talking to you
cos you never interrupt

~

DAG: (*with Angel*)

something new for our garden
fire buckets   lawn mowers   hubcaps

the bike   strap it
  to the rusty radiator
    handelbars down
      crooked wheels
        straighten 'em out
          watch 'em spin

toaster ovens   toilet seats
snow blowers   ski poles

aluminum cake plates
  to cover the hubs
    smear 'em with glue
      glue the tires
        smash a glass into confetti
          squizzle it into the glue

vacuum cleaners   bird baths
plastic peonies   soup bowls

wheels alive
  in the spokes
    jack of hearts
      ace of spades
        clikka clikka
          listen to them sing

~

MOLLY: (*spreading the word*)

    quite a collection
    you got there in your dreamland
    went to look at it yesterday afternoon
    saw the watering cans poked on a pole
    stuff dangling from their spouts
    like a hat rack
    draped my scarf on one of them

DAG:

    I know
    ya
    and thank you
    a flash of sunny shine
    orange and red
    but there it is giving it back
    it's fresh and new don't need
    bringing back to life
    got that already
    hanging on you

MOLLY:

    well let me tell you I talked to Ben
    Mister Hamburger and French Fries
    works for the newspaper
    coming to see you

DAG:

    ah no, no, no
    people read it
    they come to prowl
    if they tear it apart
    they tear apart me

MOLLY:

> nobody going to do that
> look around the garden
> just like I did
> proud of you
> happy for you
> all your hard work

DAG:

> tell him
> tell him no
> if he comes I chase him away

MOLLY:

> I told him
> you're a genius

DAG:

> well
> that's
> I suppose
> ya, but you tell him
> if he talks
> like I'm a knucklehead
> bang bang get lost

~

MOLLY: (*breakfast on the house*)

> good morning
> and here you are
> apple turnover
> milk, three sugars
> on the house

DAG:

> you don't have to
> I got
> I got two dollars

MOLLY:

> no, today is special

DAG:

> what is this?
> some kind of joke?
> everyone here smiling at me
> whooping and clapping
> you making fun of me?

MOLLY:

> I guess you haven't read it
> even got a picture of you
> take a look
> you're famous

DAG:

> well
> I don't know
> I couldn't
> I suppose
> it wouldn't
> would it
> be the end of the world
> if it's on the house
> apple turnover

MOLLY:

> cup of coffee

DAG:

> milk, three sugars

≈

DAG: (*two weeks later*)

all sorts of people
been coming to my dreamland
like this old lady in a wheelchair
think of that
in a wheelchair
I get to push and pull her
keeps taking pictures
and this man with a guitar
parked himself next to Angel
more than maybe two hours
singing all sorts of hymns
       place in my hands
       this wonderful key
and this young man blind
with somebody describing
all the treasures
and him clapping his hands
cos like he felt he could see
what's there to see

~

DAG: (*with Molly*)

> and this man in a suit and tie
> got these snakeskin slippers
> comes at me sneaky as hell
> calls it an *assemblage*
> calls it *amazing*
> I tell him I call it
> Don't Never Stop Clikka-clikking
> Gainst the Furious Wind
> but he ignores me
> calls it art
> I don't know about art
> so hoity-toity
> I call it finding something lost
> giving it new existence
> he calls it *primitive*

MOLLY:

> all right, calm down

DAG:

> give me this calling card
> some kind of museum
> where he already got something *primitive*
> from a woman in Connecticut
> builds cabins and shrines
> out of beer bottles
> ketchup and soda bottles
> a man in Washington
> gum and candy wrappers
> sheets and fragments of shiny foil
> fished out of the trashbins

wrapped around light bulbs
jelly jars and umbrellas
for some kind of throne
for God to sit on
I'm not kidding
for God, when He comes down
in some kind of
what he call it   Rapature

takes it away
my clikka clikka

MOLLY:

what are you saying
takes it away?

DAG:

what else
clikka-clikka
in his van
drives away with it
because it's *primitive*
I hate that word *primitive*
I'm not *primitive*
kept saying that
all sorts of other dingle-berry stuff
talks so fast
every time I start to say something
he keeps going
nie-yeeve effort to control
an uncoprinsible world

MOLLY:

    I think probably he means all that
    as a compliment

DAG:

    someone got snakeskin slippers
    how is that a compliment?

MOLLY:

    think of it as an honor
    your work
    in an art musem
    every day hundreds of people
    come to admire it
    he likes what you done

DAG:

    strange way of telling me

MOLLY:

    maybe he means
    primitive
    like it's from a different world
    where life isn't so complicated

DAG:

    handguns and rockets

MOLLY:

    exactly
    like what it used to be
    like
    early ancient time

DAG:

    like early ancient time
    oh, that is super joe
    early ancient time
    ya

~

DAG: (*can't wait to tell Angel*)

> this guy got snakeskin slippers
> called me *primitive*
> like early ancient time
> go down to the pond
> kneel at the edge of the water
> early ancient time
> reach with my bare hand
> to scatter the tadpoles
> and I did it
> kneeled down
> my reflection
> in the immortal stillness of the water
> my moment of looking at who I am
> okay, a long curly gray beard
> but like
> like early   ancient   time
> stuck my head in the reflection
> got myself dripping wet
> jumped up and yelled it to the sky
> I am the Wild Man of the Mountain
> I am
> Wild Man of the Mountain

~

DAG: (*a trip to Mount Washington*)

    my fingers kept time with the clatter
    cogwheel tram climbing the slope
    granite boulders hundreds of them
    huge and scratchy
    hikers bending behind them
    hiding from the wind
    rest a moment then off again
    stumbling up to the top
    never mind the grunge of the hot-dog café
    never mind the weeping mist
    makes the face feel wet
    stand together like we're in church
    looking into the distance
    at pointy peaks melting into the sky

~

DAG: (*while he was away*)

oh, Angel   somebody

             heartless dickbrains .

                 rip apart

     my timbers

                my corner posts

the tower trembles

             my lectric lights

                my Bible

               got bluestone rocks rattling
           round their stinking souls

Dad's razor Mom's necklace gone

           scatter my soap   my towel

   my socks

            shred my mattress

                     and after they

    when I come home

  in the rubble they

          I fall flat on the ground

     fold you in my arms

   ∾

MOLLY: (*late night visit*)

I find him
next to the campfire
huddled under his hood
vodka next to his knee
dark so he doesn't notice me
until I sit

try to tell him I've brought a gift
been cleaning out the kitchen
stuff I no longer need
packed into cardboard boxes

he doesn't seem to listen

I tell him
I brought the boxes up here
maybe he can use what's inside

just want to help

we sit staring into the fire
poke at it when the flame dies down
half an hour not a word

squeal of a bat flying by
pull myself up
tell him he's not alone
he's got to keep building

∽

DAG: (*as if Angel can talk*)

>louder!

>>ANGEL:

>>got to keep building

DAG:

>easy for you to say

>>ANGEL:

>>build it back

DAG:

>so somebody else can smash it down?

>>ANGEL:

>>this is nothing

DAG:

>it's everything

>>ANGEL:

>>say it, this is nothing

DAG:

>this is nothing

ANGEL:

most things break, say it

DAG:

most things break

ANGEL:

and when they do, you fix 'em

DAG:

ya, when they do, I fix 'em

∾

DAG: (*building back*)

someone with a heart of gold
dumps a broken farmer wagon
got a diesel tractor now
so no more horses needed
I strip its wheels away
settle it straight and almost level
scrounge for planks and timbers
to fashion its walls and door
a slanted roof waiting for shingles
a place for sleeping snug
until the tower's been repaired
and chant it chant it chant it
   dingdongs deadbeats
wanted to destroy me
   dickbrains dickbrains dickbrains
tried but never can

~

DAG: (*in Dreamland Garden*)

out of Molly's kitchen
I build a population
knives and spoons for fingers
toaster and wastebasket for the torso
saucepan for a hat
forks and threads from a broom
make wonderful hair
pipes and hoses become arms
legs are piled-up bowls and pots
need to find boots and slippers
for their feet
salt shaker for a nose
cup handles for ears
plates and chunks of styrofoam faces
eyes painted tight shut asleep
red and brown, white and yellow
salt & peppered with glister dust
build cabins and tables for them
gather them in groups
or place them gentle and alone
next to the wild rose bushes
friends and family for Angel
some with tears that fall in trinkles
some with a crease across their forehead
some with lips curved in smiles

~

DAG (*asleep in his farmwagon hideyhole*)

> in the stillness before the storm
> birds have been silent and flown
> trees writhe in hurricane-style winds
> rainwater thunders down the dirt road
> plunges over the edge of the cliff
> pummels and boils the pond
> brings down a massive maple
> on the half-built tower

~

DAG (*emerges from his hidey hole*
   struggles to unscramble his mind, find the energy,
  decide what he must do)

    first
        make sure the station wagon will start and check to see
        if it is damaged in any way —
    no, first
        clear scattered debris away from on top and around
        the wagon —
    no, first
        all over the garden carve a passage through the chaos
    no, first —
        because I know I will need them, I've got to recover
        all my tools from under the tree —
    no, first
        cry, wander through the garden to see how bad extensive
        the damage is —
    no, first
        find somebody willing to help me pull the tree off what's
        left of the tower —
    no, first
        find Angel, his wings, the chipped-eye smile that clung
        us together, bury what I know will be pieces —

    ~

MOLLY: (*under a moon-shy sky*)

      streetlight shadows
the village streets deserted

      cops found him
asleep in a doorway

      bundled him into the cruiser
coffee and sandwich

      bedded him down
a guest in their jail

∾

MOLLY: (*in the coffeeshop, with Dag*)

> his table occupied
> he found a spot at the counter
> across from the silver coffee urn

DAG:

> Granma had a silver coffee pot

MOLLY:

> I smile at him
> but no good morning
> busy bent over the stove
> grizzling slices of bacon

DAG:

> she hauled it out of the cupboard
> every time I went there

MOLLY:

> I take him by the elbow
> introduce him
> to sitting at his table Agatha
> social worker
> forehead locked in frowns

DAG:

> she loved to show it off
> polish it
> polish it gleaming

MOLLY:

    I push his shoulders down
    flop him into a chair
    next to Agatha

DAG:

    she banged her wheelchair always
    against the door
    I jumped up every time to help her

MOLLY:

    I can't say it
    can't tell him
    run to the kitchen
    fetch his apple turnover
    milk, three sugars

≈

MOLLY: (*stuffy smell of lemons*)

in the motel room
waiting for a bed in the nursing home
narrow-slat blinds
he's never seen anything like 'em
how they rattle open to the sunshine
stick-shape streaks on the floor
he cuts the strings
fans the slats flat on the bed
shape of a wheel
takes apart the knob
on the bathrooom door
nestles it at the center of the wheel
coat of imagined glue
sprinkles it with glister dust
transforms it
    a sunburst
       a propeller
          the eye of a hurricane
his hands grow weary
but the pulse of his magic
never stops throbbing

Note

Dag and Molly are fictional characters. Dag got his name after I found, in the *OED*, that it's a word with multiple meanings, among them, 1. an extraordinary and admirable person, or, 2. slang for a socially inept or awkward person. I imagine a family, unaware of #1, so often abusively calling him #2, it became his name.

About the Author

Tony Howarth, editor for dramatic writing with *The Westchester Review*, is a playwright, director, former journalist, retired in 1991 after 28 years as a high school and college teacher of English and theatre. William Wordsworth helped him survive adolescence, inspired him to write poetry of his own, but as a college freshman he found a sense sublime of something far more deeply interfused did not fit well in a climate devoted to the work of Eliot and Pope. He adjusted his ambitions to journalism, in Cleveland, Meriden CT, the U.S. Army, Lancaster PA, Indianapolis, and New York City where he was editor of the editorial page of *The World-Telegram and Sun*. Disillusioned after a printers' strike and the assasination of John F. Kennedy, he turned to teaching, where he was asked to develop a theatre program, which in turn led to a list of professional credits, including a dozen plays and a musical presented off-Broadway; full lengths include *Thornwood*, which won a Drama League grant, produced at Circle Rep and the Mint Theatre in New York City, colleges across the U.S., Amsterdam, Tanzania, made into an award-winning indie film, *Slings and Arrows*. For many summers he directed musicals at the College Light Opera Company in Falmouth MA. He began writing poetry again in 2009 after a visit to Wordworth's Dove Cottage (clouds and daffodils) in England's Lake District. His poetry, developed at the Hudson Valley Writing Center under the treasured guidance of Jennifer Franklin and Fred Marchant, has appeared in many magazines, among them *Chronogram*, *The Naugatuck River Review*, a magazine in England *Obsessed with Pipework*, *The Connecticut River Review*, *Raven's Perch*, *The Sow's Ear*, and the Grayson Press anthology *Forgotten Women*. And a play published by *The Westchester Review* called *The Wedding Ring*, a moment in the life of who else but William Wordsworth.